Lucretia Rudolph Garfield

Lucretia Rudolph Garfield

* * * * * * * * * * * * * * * * * * * *

1832–1918

BY ANN HEINRICHS

CHILDREN'S PRESS®
A Division of Grolier Publishing
New York London Hong Kong Sydney
Danbury, Connecticut

Consultants:	F. SUZANNE MILLER
	Curator, The Western Reserve
	Historical Society,
	James A. Garfield National
	Historic Site, "Lawnfield"
	LINDA CORNWELL
	Learning Resource Consultant
	Indiana Department of Education

Project Editor:	DOWNING PUBLISHING SERVICES
Page Layout:	CAROLE DESNOES
Photo Researcher:	JAN IZZO

Visit Children's Press on the Internet at:
http://publishing.grolier.com

Library of Congress Cataloging-in-Publication Data
Heinrichs, Ann
     Lucretia Rudolph Garfield, 1832–1918 / by Ann Heinrichs
        p. cm. — (Encyclopedia of first ladies)
     Includes bibliographical references and index.
     Summary: A biography of the wife of the twentieth president of the United
States, who became widely admired for her intelligence and strong convictions.
     ISBN 0-516-20846-2
     1. Garfield, Lucretia Rudolph, 1832–1918—Juvenile literature. 2. Presidents' spouses—
United States—Biography—Juvenile literature. [1. Garfield, Lucretia Rudolph, 1832–1918.
2. First ladies. 3. Women—Biography.] I. Title
E687.2.H45   1998
973.8'4'092—dc21   97–47279
[B]   CIP
                                          AC

Table of Contents

Lucretia Rudolph Garfield

CHAPTER ONE

"Dear Wife"

✫ ✫ ✫ ✫ ✫ ✫ ✫ ✫ ✫ ✫ ✫ ✫ ✫ ✫ ✫ ✫ ✫

"Dear Wife," the telegram began. Lucretia Garfield, in the parlor of their Ohio farmhouse, studied James's words. Only a week before, he had boarded a train for Chicago. There, at the Republican National Convention, he gave a speech to nominate another man for president. She read on:

"If the result meets your approval I shall be content. Love to all the household."

Lucretia knew what "the result" was. James himself had just become the Republican candidate for president of the United States.

"When the telegram came," she later wrote, "I did

✫ ✫ ✫ ✫ ✫ ✫ ✫ ✫ ✫ ✫ ✫ ✫ ✫ ✫ ✫ ✫

not know whether to be sad or rejoice." Maybe she remembered what James had said many years before: "I hope and believe that I shall never be smitten with the presidential disease. . . . I think it is better to deserve the place than to reach it."

Five months later, as chill November winds whipped around the farmhouse, Lucretia warmed herself by the fire. Around the room, family, friends, and neighbors were chatting excitedly, for another telegram had arrived. This one revealed that James had won the election.

Shy, private, and plainly dressed, Lucretia was used to staying in the background. Now she was to be First

What's in a Name?

☆ ☆

> Again a Mary? Nay, Lucretia,
> The noble, classic name
> That well Befits our fair ladie,
> Our sweet and gentle dame. . . .

begins a poem written by a poet from the college that both Lucretia and James attended. Classical names such as Lucretia, taken from ancient Greek and Roman culture and literature, were fairly common in their day, especially among the upper class. Cornelius, Eugene, and Ulysses are other examples. The Bible has also been a ready source of names. Lucretia's father's name, Zebulon, is not only biblical but fitting to a carpenter for it means "dwelling." Other trends in naming sprang from more popular sources such as current novels. Today, children's names are often inspired by popular culture. Many girls born in the 1930s were named for the popular child star Shirley Temple. In the 1970s, parents inspired by soap operas often named their children after favorite characters.

Lady. With her romantic imagination, she must have pictured what the future held in store—the White House, decked with flowers and brilliant with lights; receptions, dinners, and balls; and herself, the gracious hostess in elegant gowns, moving among her guests with style and grace.

All these visions would come true. Yet there was one thing Lucretia could never have imagined. An unspeakable tragedy would shatter her life to the core. The very next winter would find her far from the White House—no longer First Lady, but a private citizen cloaked in grief.

☆ ☆ ☆ ☆ ☆ ☆ ☆ ☆ ☆ ☆ ☆ ☆ ☆ ☆ ☆

CHAPTER TWO

Growing Up in the Western Reserve

☆ ☆ ☆ ☆ ☆ ☆ ☆ ☆ ☆ ☆ ☆ ☆ ☆ ☆ ☆ ☆ ☆

Zebulon Rudolph and Arabella Mason grew up as pioneers. They settled in northeastern Ohio Territory, in a region called the Western Reserve. After they married, Zeb and Arabella built a cabin in the village of Garrettsville. An expert carpenter, Zeb found plenty of work building houses and barns for other families in the area. Lucretia, their first child, was born on April 19, 1832.

The Rudolphs, like many other Western Reserve families, were members of the Disciples of Christ Church. The Disciples believed in freedom of religious thought. They saw the Bible as their only authority.

☆ ☆ ☆ ☆ ☆ ☆ ☆ ☆ ☆ ☆ ☆ ☆ ☆ ☆ ☆ ☆ ☆

Portrait of America, 1832: *Land of Liberty*

✩ ✩ ✩ ✩ ✩ ✩ ✩ ✩ ✩ ✩ ✩ ✩ ✩ ✩ ✩ ✩ ✩ ✩ ✩ ✩

By 1832, the year of Lucretia's birth, an America we might recognize today was beginning to take shape. By then, the nation included twenty-four states and nearly 14 million people. Andrew Jackson, the first Democratic president, was about to serve his second term and a spirit of democracy swept the land. War hero Jackson fired the common people's imaginations and encouraged ordinary Americans to take part and take pride in their country. In this land of opportunity, anyone could succeed. The "self-made man" came to represent the American ideal. For the first time, books, plays, and music were written for a popular audience. The right to vote, once based on property ownership, was now extended to nearly all white males. To the bewilderment of European visitors who were used to distinct class differences, Americans cherished the notion of equality. "My country 'tis of thee, sweet land of liberty," they sang in the year's most popular song, *America*.

This rising spirit of equality, however, only emphasized the plight of those who were not considered equal under the law: women, black slaves, and Native Americans.

Laws restricting the lives of slaves were in fact tightened; it is no wonder that an organized movement to abolish slavery began to emerge. Even that movement was run by men, however, and women were growing resentful that the battle for equal rights did not extend to them.

For Native Americans, especially those who lived in the East and Southeast, this was a sad year. So anxious were white Americans to settle the land they occupied that conflicts arose about who should govern the tribes. Finally, a bill passed in 1830 dictated the "removal" of tribes to lands west of the Mississippi River. Many Indians resisted leaving their farmlands, and the Black Hawk War erupted in Illinois as the displaced Sauk and Fox tried to return there.

Many of the contradictions of 1832 remain with us today.

This picture of the four Rudolph children was taken about 1855. Left to right, from youngest to oldest: Ellen, Joseph, John, and Lucretia

Zeb, who was an outspoken church leader, often preached at Sunday services. Lucretia grew up hearing Bible stories. In time, she learned to read them herself.

Like all pioneer children, she helped out with house and farm chores. These included canning fruit, baking bread, weaving cloth, and salting meat for winter storage. Lucretia was a shy and serious girl. Family and friends called her by the nickname "Crete." Her closest friend, Lizzie Atwood, was the only one with whom she shared her secrets and dreams.

The Rudolphs had three more children—John, Joseph, and Ellen. In raising her children, Arabella stressed the virtue of "self-government." Neither parent showed affection

Ohio, U.S.A.

✱ ✱

One corner of Ohio was once a part of Connecticut! After the American Revolution, many of the original thirteen states claimed lands in the unexplored West. Part of Connecticut's claim included a 3.5-million-acre (1.4-million-hectare) triangle of land between Lake Erie and Pennsylvania's western border. This region became known as the Western Reserve, and much of it was settled by New Englanders, who founded Cleveland in 1796. Connecticut gave up the Western Reserve in 1800, and it became part of the new state of Ohio in 1803. The state (whose name comes from the Iroquois word for "beautiful") extends from Lake Erie on the north to the Ohio River Valley on the south. Throughout Lucretia's childhood, the good land continued to attract many farmers from the East, where they had exhausted much of the soil. So many came, in fact, that by the late 1830s, Ohio led the nation in wheat production, and the landscape teemed with travelers. Canals, wagon trails, rivers, and the first horse-drawn railroad brought many of them west. Others followed the National Road, which connected Maryland and Illinois through Ohio by 1838. Today, Highway 40 still traces its path across the southern half of the state.

openly. Lucretia later remembered that her mother kissed her only once in a while. She did not remember ever being kissed by her father.

Winters in northeast Ohio were snowy and bitterly cold. Lucretia, delicate and small for her age, had problems with her lungs. In wintertime and early spring, she had a racking cough. Often it caused a pain in her right side.

When Lucretia was sixteen, Zeb decided to enroll her in Geauga Seminary. Geauga was a sort of high school in Chester, Ohio, about 30 miles (48 kilometers) from the Rudolphs' home. Zeb hooked up a carriage, and together they rode through

16

This lovely section of Ohio's beautiful Chagrin River Valley is not far from Geauga Seminary, where Lucretia's father enrolled her when she was sixteen years old.

hills and forestland into the Chagrin River Valley.

The town of Chester was just a handful of houses and a general store. High on a sloping ridge stood the three-story wooden school building of Geauga Seminary. On top was a square cupola, or dome. Around the building was a picket fence.

Lucretia had never been away from home before. She must have been just a little nervous as she walked up the gravel path to the schoolhouse door. Inside, she found a library, a large salon, a chapel with benches and a podium, and several classrooms. On the top floor were tiny rooms where the students lived.

Students at Geauga wore their Sunday clothes every day. They were called "Mr." and "Miss" instead of their first names. No dancing or drinking was allowed. On Saturday, after chapel service, students took turns speaking at the podium. Some recited famous speeches or poems, and others recited their own works.

Tuition was three dollars for twelve weeks of basic courses. Adding higher-level courses could bring the fee up to four dollars. This was a large sum at the time. In those days, a full day of hard labor could earn fifty to seventy-five cents. Geauga offered classes in Latin and Greek classics, as well as English grammar and composition. Algebra, geometry, and natural sciences were taught, too.

In science class, Lucretia couldn't help noticing an awkward young man named Mr. Garfield. She found him to be a "strange genius" who made "odd remarks." The other students, she said, had him "singled out for a prodigy." Yet it was Albert Hall who captured her heart. Maybe she admired Albert's quick mind. Or maybe it was his darkly handsome looks and his fashionable clothes. In any case, everyone knew that Lucretia and Albert were an "item."

In the spring, the students went on field trips. They would spend the day at another school in the area or visit some spot with beautiful scenery. They were to write about their experiences in their composition books, using all they had learned in their classes. Thus, Lucretia described one spring day this way:

"Cloudless dawned the morning of May 19, 1849, and when Phoebus from behind the curtained east, came forth clad in all his glory, and commenced his daily circuit through the azure deep, radiant with joy were our many faces in anticipation of that day." In today's terms, Lucretia might have written, "It was a sunny day, and we felt really good."

James Garfield at the age of sixteen

In June 1850, at age eighteen, Lucretia graduated from Geauga Seminary. She returned to Garrettsville and kept in touch with Albert Hall through letters.

A Sailor's Life

✩ ✩

At the age of sixteen, his imagination full of scenes from a book entitled *The Pirate's Own Book*, James left home to become a sailor. He journeyed to Cleveland, but was refused employment by a rude Lake Erie ship's captain. Garfield then decided to try another approach to the sea: he found work driving mules for a canal boat on the Ohio and Pennsylvania Canal. He worked hard and got along well with the other boatmen and was soon made bowman. A biographer writing in 1881 told how this career came to an end: "One night as the boat approached a lock the bowman was hastily awakened, and tumbled out half asleep

James Garfield grew up in this cabin in Cuyahoga County, Ohio.

to attend to his duty. Uncoiling a rope which was to assist in steadying the boat through, he lost his balance, and in a second found himself in a now familiar place at the bottom of the canal. The night was dark, and no help near. Struggling about, his hand accidentally clutched a section of the rope which had gone over with him. . . . The rope slid off; swim he could not. Jerk, jerk; the rope has caught. Pulling away with a will, he climbed back to his place, and found that he had been saved by a splinter in a plank in which the rope had caught by a knot. Might not this be in answer to a mother's prayer? Was it possible that he had been saved for some better fortune than his present life promised? When the boat neared home again, James bade good-bye to the *Evening Star*." For James, the next adventure from home would be to Geauga Seminary.

James Garfield at the age of fourteen

Garfield as a canal-boat boy

CHAPTER THREE

College Days and Romance

Zeb Rudolph and other elders in the Disciples of Christ had grand plans. They built a college in Hiram, a few miles from Garrettsville. It was called the Western Reserve Eclectic Institute, or the Eclectic for short.

Zeb believed it would be good for his children to live near a college community. He built a rambling seven-room house on Hiram Hill, overlooking the campus. Then he and Arabella packed up their family and their household goods and moved to Hiram.

The red-brick college building stood in an open field. On top was a zinc-covered dome that could be

Educating American Women: A Timeline

✦ ✦

1645 Massachusetts governor William Bradford explains that constant reading and writing have caused his wife's madness: "Such things as are proper for men whose minds are stronger." *1655* In Massachusetts, 50 percent of women are illiterate, 60 percent in New York, and 75 percent in Virginia. *1688* In Farmington, Connecticut, taxpayers decide that only boys shall be allowed at the common school. *1746* Moravian Women's Seminary, the first girl's boarding school, opens. *1751–1820* Life of Judith Sargent Murray. Considered the first American feminist, she writes that girls should be better taught so as to achieve financial independence. *1821* Emma Willard establishes Troy Female Seminary in New York, the first endowed girls' school. *1826* The first public high schools for girls open in New York and Boston. *1833* Oberlin College is the first institution of higher learning chartered to be coeducational. *1850* Coed Western Reserve Eclectic Institute opens for its first term. *1853* Susan B. Anthony is the first woman to speak before the New York State Teachers' Convention. *1870* Chemist and home economist Ellen Swallow Richards is the first woman accepted at Massachusetts Institute of Technology (MIT). *1875* Smith and Wellesley women's colleges are founded. *1878* Women are accepted at MIT on an equal basis with men. *1879* Businesswoman Mary Seymour establishes the first typewriting school for women, opening the male-dominated field of clerical work to women. *1879* Scientist Elizabeth Agassiz cofounds Radcliffe College and acts as president. *1881* Sophia Packard and Harriet Giles open Spelman College for black women in Atlanta. *1921* About 283,000 women enroll in college, amounting to 47 percent of total enrollment. *1973* Lynn Genesko, a swimmer at the University of Miami, receives the first athletic scholarship given to a woman. *1978* Hannah H. Gray of the University of Chicago becomes the first female university president. *1984* Kristine Holderied graduates top in her class at the U.S. Naval Academy, the first woman midshipman to do so.

seen from miles away. Newly planted trees dotted the school grounds, though they were too small to provide much shade.

The Eclectic was one of the first colleges in the country to admit both men and women. The idea of coed colleges was radical at the time. Some people believed that women had inferior minds. They felt that mixing men and women would lower the standards for achievement. Others saw men and women as mentally equal. Some even argued that women would raise a school's moral standards and improve the men's behavior.

Lucretia enrolled in the Eclectic's first term in 1850. She planned to become a teacher. At 8:00 every morning, students assembled in a hall called the Lower Chapel. The schoolmaster led Bible readings and prayers, then classes began. Courses at the Eclectic were much like those at Geauga, only more difficult. Many students, including Lucretia, sang in the glee club. Lucretia herself helped start a group called the Ladies' Literary Society.

James Garfield enrolled in the Eclectic, too. To help pay his way, he worked as a janitor. He chopped wood for the stoves, swept rooms, and rang the big bell in the schoolhouse tower. One girl wrote, "His clothes had a poor-student look." James was 6 feet (183 centimeters) tall, with broad shoulders. His thick, bushy, light-brown hair was cut short, so that it stood almost straight up. Beneath this shock of hair was a pair of piercing blue eyes.

By the end of 1851, Lucretia had lost faith in Albert Hall. On New Year's Eve, she broke up with him. "I saw no hope of his ever becoming a Christian," she wrote. "I ought never to have loved him, but for some reason—I know not what—I did. I believed his character was good."

Albert had been the love of Lucretia's life. She had believed they would be married someday. Now she was in agony. Turning to God, she prayed that her "evil propensities" would go away. More than ever, she buried herself in her studies.

In the spring of 1853, Lucretia's Greek teacher became ill. James Garfield, far ahead of the other students,

In this group picture of Western Reserve Eclectic Institute students, James is on the far left and Lucretia is on the far right.

stepped in to teach in his place. James, too, had recently broken up with someone. Now, he began to notice Miss Lucretia Rudolph. By this time, she had grown into a pretty young lady—small and delicate with high cheekbones and dark, shiny hair. Behind her dark, deep-set eyes was a brilliant, curious mind. At five feet, three inches (160 cm) tall, she was tiny compared to James, who was six feet (183 cm) tall.

At first, James was more interested in a romance than Lucretia was. When it was time for the class picture, James took the photographer aside. Make sure you seat Miss Rudolph next to me, he told him. As instructed,

When it was time for the Eclectic class picture to be taken in April 1853, James (right front) made sure the photographer seated him next to Lucretia.

Lucretia shrank timidly into her place beside the brawny Mr. Garfield.

For their graduation program in June, the students put on a play. It was about the Bible characters King Ahasuerus and Queen Esther. James and Lucretia played the starring roles. One day during rehearsal, Lucretia was walking backstage. All of a sudden she stumbled and began to fall. A pair of strong arms caught her just in time. It was James. For a moment their eyes met, and "a strange wild delight thrilled my soul," she later wrote. But the next moment, she wriggled out of his grasp and "darted quickly away."

In the fall, Lucretia taught school in the nearby town of Chagrin Falls.

The Lure of Niagara

✫ ✫

The immense cascade of water called Niagara Falls has fascinated human beings since they first laid eyes on it several centuries ago. Over the falls, the Niagara River plunges 180 feet (55 meters) to the gorge below in a chaotic torrent of crashing water that fills the air with spray, mist, and a thundering roar. Native Americans and early explorers marveled at the waterfall's great power; later visitors found the scene hard to describe in its scale and beauty. Half in Canada and half in the United States, Niagara Falls shortly became one of North America's first tourist attractions. As vacationing became popular in the 1800s, travelers flocked to the site. The first hotels were built in the 1820s. Hucksters, cheap souvenir vendors, high-priced tour guides, and dime museums soon followed. But none could overcome the grandeur of the sight. Women often fainted in its presence, and its hypnotic power lured many to death over its brink. By the time James Garfield visited the falls in 1853, more than 50,000 visitors made the trip each

year. The falls rapidly built a reputation as a haven for honeymooners and daredevils. Several years after James's visit, the extraordinary "rope dancer" Charles Blondin cooked omelets on a small stove teetering atop a tightrope high over the gorge while crowds of spectators looked on.

On weekends, she came home to Hiram. One day in November, she was surprised to find a letter waiting for her. It was from James, who was vacationing at Niagara Falls, New York. These shimmering waterfalls were among the most popular tourist attractions in America.

"Lucretia My Sister," it began. James rambled on and on describing his beautiful surroundings. Then he wrote about the value of studying Greek and Latin classics. He invited Lucretia to write and share her opinions, too.

Lucretia was nervous about writing back. Nevertheless, she sent a long reply, beginning with "Very Kind Brother." She said that she doubted the value of studying the classics too heavily. A person's time might be better spent on "pursuits more worthy." Even after James was back in town, the letter writing continued.

In his diary, James debated with himself about Lucretia. He felt that she was not very ambitious and not very warm. For another thing, she enjoyed hearing women's speeches at school. This worried James. It could mean that she was in favor of women's rights. In his mind, women did not belong in public life. On the other hand, she was a good Christian. When he looked at the big picture, this was the most important thing.

At the time, it was not proper for a couple to be alone together unless they were officially "courting." But James found his chance. In February 1854, he persuaded Lucretia to meet him in the college's Lower Chapel. For the first time, the two had a private talk.

James said he wished that they could get to know each other better. Lucretia agreed; she would like that, too. He held her close, and they exchanged their first kiss. Lucretia later described the "icy coldness with which [the kiss] was received." At this early stage, she said, James had not yet "reached the heart."

After this meeting, Lucretia and James—in today's terms—were "going steady." They met often, reading poems and stories to each other and taking walks.

At Lucretia's graduation in June, she was the only woman to give a

The Rules of Love

★ ★ ★ ★ ★ ★ ★ ★ ★ ★ ★ ★ ★ ★ ★ ★ ★ ★ ★ ★

Even though the etiquette (or manners) of official courting permitted James and Lucretia to be alone together, it allowed little else. For example, on a country walk, if the young lady wished to sit and rest, the gentleman could not sit next to her but must remain standing. A gentleman could not offer his arm in the daytime to anyone but his fiancée. At night or where footing was unsure, the rule relaxed to allow a man to assist any female. The respectability of kissing before marriage was hotly debated. Some advisors felt it too large a risk, since engagements did sometimes break off. In general, Victorian manners disapproved of any public display of affection. Even married couples were advised to "treat each other, in all outward forms, and in all true respect and courtesy, as if they were not married."

speech. "Commerce" was her topic. Now she wondered what to do next. She and James would probably get married one day. Yet, she truly loved reading, studying, and translating Greek and Latin texts.

Naturally, she wrote her thoughts to James. If married, she wrote, "I know not why I might not still study. True, it has become almost a proverb that when a lady is married, she may as well lay aside her books, still I do not believe it contains very much wisdom after all."

James believed it was better for women to study a mixture of languages, music, and art. "The female mind," he said, "should be ornamented, as well as strengthened." Lucretia thanked him for his advice. "Woman's province is her home," she wrote. "Let woman's brightest rays be shed upon her own household, and her words of deepest eloquence fall by her own fireside."

As for himself, James felt he needed more education. In July 1854, he left for Williams College in Williamstown, Massachusetts. Meanwhile, Lucretia taught at the Eclectic

The Williams College Library, in Williamstown, Massachusetts

Williamstown as it looked about the time James attended college there

31

This picture of James Garfield was probably taken during the time he was principal of the Eclectic.

and took piano lessons. The next year, she accepted a teaching job in nearby Ravenna, Ohio. There she taught French, arithmetic, algebra, and reading. In their letters, she and James began calling each other by the nicknames "Crete" and "Jamie." After he graduated from Williams in 1856, James came back to Hiram and became principal of the Eclectic.

In those days, couples were sometimes engaged for years. As time went on, though, Lucretia began to wonder when they would marry. James seemed to be in no hurry. In his diary, he called marriage a "lottery business." To him, marriage seemed like a big gamble. Maybe Lucretia would be a good mate, but maybe not.

Lucretia herself was not sure that she would be happy as a wife. As it was, she enjoyed teaching and earning money of her own. James had seemed cold and unfriendly since he'd returned from college. Worst of all, she found that he had grown close to another woman, Rebecca Selleck, while he was away. Miserable and confused, Lucretia told James that if he wanted to marry Rebecca, he was free to go. Then she took off for a teaching job in Cleveland.

The bustling city of Cleveland was a refreshing change for Lucretia. Euclid Avenue, its main street, was known as "Millionaires' Row." Up and down the avenue were ornate mansions and lavish gardens. Gaslights lined the paved streets. Lucretia discovered that she loved attending

Cleveland, a lovely and bustling city, was a refreshing change for Lucretia, who had spent her life in rural northeastern Ohio.

Mansions like this one lined Cleveland's Euclid Avenue, which was known as "Millionaires' Row."

James and Lucretia were married in the home Zeb Rudolph had built on Hiram Hill, overlooking the Eclectic campus.

plays. She also took painting, drawing, and music classes.

Cleveland's schools were in the midst of a crisis. Second- and third-grade students had trouble reading first-grade books. The superintendent decided that all students should go back to their first-grade readers again. They should drill and drill until they really knew how to read.

At Brownell Street public school, Lucretia was eager to carry out the plan. "I love my little school very much," she wrote. "I try to teach the children only a very few things, but try to make those few thoroughly understood and leave them firmly impressed."

More than a year passed. James had run out of ideas about what to do or why. Finally, on a buggy ride in April 1858, he proposed and Lucretia accepted. It was not a romantic scene, though. James spoke of their marriage as the right thing to do. Probably, too, as principal of the Eclectic, James wanted to stay in the good graces of Lucretia's father.

As the wedding day drew closer, James did not seem much warmer. Lucretia wrote, "There are hours when my heart almost breaks with the cruel thought that our marriage is based upon the cold stern word *duty*." Her family even worried that he might not show up. At her brother's suggestion, Lucretia mailed James an invitation to his own wedding.

On November 11, 1858, the couple was married in a small ceremony in the Rudolphs' home. Lucretia wore a simple white gown with lace around the neck. Several girls from the college were bridesmaids and served refreshments. "We were dressed in white, with low necks and short sleeves," one of them wrote. Another guest reported that "the bride and her maids were a galaxy of beauty." At the wedding supper, Lucretia took part in a tradition called "cutting the bride's loaf."

The newlyweds did not have enough money to buy a house, or even to rent one. Instead, they moved into a rooming house on campus and began their life together. Lucretia was now a middle-class housewife.

☆　☆　☆　☆　☆　☆　☆　☆　☆　☆　☆　☆　☆　☆

CHAPTER FOUR

More Than a Clinging Vine

* * * * * * * * * * * * * * * * * * * *

After the American Revolution, married women often moved out of the homes and communities where they grew up. This left them without support and advice about homemaking. Catharine Beecher's *Treatise on Domestic Economy* helped fill the gap. It was the most popular handbook for housewives in the mid-1800s. At just fifty cents, it was inexpensive enough for almost anyone to buy.

In plain language, Beecher explained the mysteries of cooking, table setting, child care, cleanliness, and first aid. She also insisted that men and women were equals. It was only for the good of society that

* * * * * * * * * * * * * * * * * * *

When James won a seat in the Ohio State Senate, he moved to Columbus without Lucretia.

women took care of the home. She painted the woman's role as highly romantic.

Lucretia seems to have shared this view. James once described himself as the "sturdy oak" and Lucretia as the "clinging vine" twined around it. "I loved the comparison," she said. Married life for her was a "deep untold joy." She would soon find marriage to be as rocky as courtship had been. And James would find that she was much more than a "clinging vine."

In January 1860, James won a seat in the Ohio State Senate. Off he went to live in Columbus, the state capital. Lucretia missed him terribly. He rarely came home, and he discouraged her from visiting. He told her that their marriage was probably a big mistake. After they made up, she promised, "I am going to try harder than ever before to be the best little wife possible." In July, Lucretia gave birth to a baby girl, Eliza. She and James nicknamed her "Little Trot," after a character in the Charles Dickens book *David Copperfield.*

Eliza "Little Trot" Garfield

Author Charles Dickens

Charles Dickens (1812–1870)

☆ ☆

English author Charles Dickens wrote stories about the London he saw. His works, including *David Copperfield,* explore the hardships of England's industrial way of life and the human suffering in London's orphanages and asylums. During his visit to America in 1842, Dickens visited wealthy households as well as slums, prisons, factories, and plantations. *American Notes,* the work he published that fall, made British fans chuckle over its portrayal of America, both good and bad. Criticism by a foreign visitor, however, displeased Americans. After the Civil War, America and Dickens made up. He accepted invitations to return, and wrote, "The people here know how to treat a guest." American poet Henry Wadsworth Longfellow observed at Dickens's death that "the whole country is stricken with grief." Apparently, the Garfields were not the only fans of Dickens's work.

President Abraham Lincoln and his wife, Mary Todd Lincoln

One day in Columbus, James saw Abraham Lincoln, the newly elected president. He wrote to Lucretia that Lincoln was "distressedly homely. But through all his awkward homeliness there is a look of transparent, genuine goodness." He did not speak so kindly about First Lady Mary Todd Lincoln: "His wife is a stocky, sallow, pugnosed plain lady." Lucretia scolded him for judging Mrs. Lincoln only on appearances.

Meanwhile, around the country, war was brewing. Northern and

When Confederate troops fired on Fort Sumter in April 1861, the Civil War began.

Brigadier General James Garfield (front center) with other officers of the 42nd Ohio Volunteer Regiment

Southern states argued viciously about whether slavery should be allowed. Eleven Southern states seceded, or pulled away from the Union, to form the Confederate States of America. In April 1861, Confederate troops fired on Fort Sumter in South Carolina. With these shots, America's Civil War began.

James signed up to serve in the Union army. He was opposed to slav-ery and alarmed that the nation was breaking in two. Leading his 42nd Ohio Volunteer Regiment, he marched off to war. Lucretia and Little Trot moved back in with her parents. In 1862, a severe fever sent James home to recover his health. He, Lucretia, and Trot went away for a restful vacation. The trip did wonders for the Garfields' relationship. "Our love is perfect," Lucretia wrote, "and all is peace."

In October, Ohio voters elected James to the U.S. House of Repre-sentatives. What he wanted most of all, though, was to return to army duty. Leaving his family behind, he traveled to Washington, D.C., to re-quest another assignment. At once, he was caught up in the political in-trigues of the nation's capital. When Christmas came, he was too busy to go home.

Lucretia felt that James was ignor-ing his family. She had just rented a little house for them across from the college campus. With fierce bargain-ing, she got it for $100 a year. Then she scurried about, buying furniture and fixing it up. She wanted to make

The Civil War: Fast Facts

WHAT: The War between the States

WHEN: 1861–1865

WHO: Between the Union (Northern states) and the Confederacy (Southern states)

WHERE: Battles were fought as far north as Pennsylvania, south to Florida, and west into Missouri

WHY: Many complicated reasons contributed to the outbreak of civil war. Basic differences between the economies and ways of life in the North and the South led to disagreements over slavery and the power of states versus the power of the federal government. When the Southern states left the Union to form their own government, war soon followed.

OUTCOME: After a devastating loss of American life, Northern and Southern, the Union won the war largely because the South ran out of supplies, men, and energy. Slavery was abolished, and the Confederate states returned to the Union.

As soon as James returned to Hiram in January 1863 and saw the house Lucretia had rented, he was so delighted that he bought it on the spot.

it a warm and cozy home in time for the holidays. Now there was no James to share it with her. She wrote an icy letter, calling him cold and thoughtless.

James made it home in January 1863. He was so thrilled with the house that he bought it on the spot for $825. Right away, he set off for his new army post. He was to join General William Rosecrans in Tennessee. There he fought in the Battle of Chickamauga and rose from the rank of brigadier general to major general. Lucretia learned that Albert Hall, her first love, had also led an Ohio regiment in the war. He died of a bullet wound to the head.

In October, Lucretia had a baby boy, Harry Augustus. James, discharged from the army, headed back to Washington to take up his seat in

"A Mad, Irregular Battle"

★ ★

The Battle of Chickamauga was one of several to be fought around Chattanooga, Tennessee, in the fall of 1863. Although that battle itself was a crushing defeat for the Union army, the campaign eventually led to the retreat of the Confederate army and the capture of the critical rail hub of Chattanooga by Union forces. On September 19 and 20, 1863, at Chickamauga—10 miles (16 km) south of Chattanooga—Union troops were unable to hold off the Confederates, who trapped them and cut off their supplies. Losses were devastating in this vicious two-day battle, totaling 16,000 Union casualties and 18,000 Confederate. The heroics of General George Thomas, who held his position while Commanding General William Rosecrans fled, earned him the nickname "the Rock of Chickamauga." As chief of staff under Rosecrans, James Garfield (the youngest brigadier general

Congress. Again, Lucretia began to feel as if she had no husband. She had been keeping track of their living arrangements. In five years of marriage, she told James, they had actually lived together for only twenty weeks.

In November, three-year-old Trot came down with diphtheria. This was a common childhood disease caused by bacteria. Today, parents can have their children vaccinated to prevent it. But in the 1860s, French chemist Louis Pasteur was still working on his brand-new idea that germs cause diseases. It would be fifty years before

in the Union army) conducted his own heroics by delivering a message to Thomas under heavy fire. After the defeat, Thomas replaced Rosecrans and by November, Chattanooga was won. Garfield earned a promotion to major general.

vaccinations were introduced. Crazed with worry, James rushed home. On December 2, the child died.

James began to realize that he and his family needed to live together. He rented a three-story brick house in Washington. For Lucretia's convenience, there was a water hydrant just outside the kitchen door. Now the Garfields lived in Washington from November through March, while Congress was in session. Then they spent their summers in Hiram. Two more babies joined the family—James in 1865 and Mollie in 1867.

By the end of the 1867 session,

James needed a rest. He persuaded Lucretia to join him on a trip to Europe. After Lucretia arranged to have the children cared for in their absence, they set sail across the Atlantic. In four months, they breezed

The Garfields' residence in Washington, D.C.

Louis Pasteur (1822–1895)

★ ★ ★ ★ ★ ★ ★ ★ ★ ★ ★ ★ ★ ★ ★ ★ ★ ★ ★ ★

Can you imagine living in a world with no germs? Before Louis Pasteur made his many great discoveries, people did not understand that such living microorganisms existed. No one knew why yeast made bread rise or why sugary fluids could turn to alcohol. People thought disease was caused by bad air, rather than by actual living microbes. Worst of all, doctors didn't realize how important it was to keep their hands and instruments clean. By discovering the secrets of germs, Louis Pasteur gave us the two greatest defenses against them: cleanliness and germs themselves. Pasteur found that when given a weakened form of a specific germ, the body learns to recognize and fight the full-strength germ more efficiently. This is how vaccinations work against some diseases.

46

through England, Scotland, Belgium, Germany, Switzerland, France, and Italy. The trip was good medicine for their sagging marriage. In Lucretia's words, it "deepened and perfected" their love.

Among the places the Garfields visited during their trip through Europe were Edinburgh, Scotland (above); Antwerp, Belgium (below); Berlin, Germany (above right); and Rome, Italy (right).

CHAPTER FIVE

A Home, a Farm, and a Cow

★ ★ ★ ★ ★ ★ ★ ★ ★ ★ ★ ★ ★ ★ ★ ★

James was determined to give his family a permanent home in Washington. He bought a plot of land at 13th and I Streets and hired carpenters to build a house. In the autumn of 1869, Lucretia was delighted to move into their very own house in the capital.

One by one, new little Garfields arrived—Irvin in 1870, Abram in 1872, and Edward, called Ned, in 1874. The growing family could no longer fit in their summer house in Hiram. Besides, it was badly in need of repairs. Sadly, Lucretia and James sold the house that had been their first real home. Then they spent summers with the Rudolphs or in rented cottages.

★ ★ ★ ★ ★ ★ ★ ★ ★ ★ ★ ★ ★ ★ ★ ★

After the Garfields sold their house in Hiram, they spent summers with the Rudolphs. The extended family, including James, Lucretia, and their children, is shown here during the summer of 1874.

James became quite an important person in the House of Representatives. He was chairman of the Appropriations Committee, which made decisions about government spending. Later, he was House minority leader. Although he was respected, things did not always go smoothly for him.

Congressman Oakes Ames ran a company called Crédit Mobilier. This company was building the nation's transcontinental railroad. Ames sold shares in the company to other con-

Congressman Oakes Ames

From Sea to Shining Sea

✯ ✯

At the end of the Civil War, railroads extended only as far west as Omaha, Nebraska. As the population of the West grew, the time came to connect California with the East Coast. Begun in 1866, the transcontinental railroad was a tremendous feat of construction accomplished largely by Chinese and Irish immigrants. They built one line west from Omaha and the other line east from California. Through the snowy mountains, over deep canyons, and across dusty plains, workers raced to connect the two lines in Utah. Crews on the Union Pacific line covered nearly 1,000 miles (1,609 km) in three years. Made up of former soldiers from both sides of the Civil War, freed slaves, and thousands of Irish immigrants, the Union Pacific team crossed the Great Plains and climbed the highest point any railroad had then reached in the world, Sherman Summit. But the workers on the Central Pacific line—most of whom were Chinese immigrants—set the record, laying ten miles (16 km) of track in one day,

an effort that involved driving 120,000 spikes into 31,000 ties! They blasted fifteen tunnels through granite mountains, braved avalanches, and sweated their way across the desert. Finally, on May 10, 1869, the two lines met, with much celebration, at Promontory, Utah.

Congressman James Garfield (right) was an influential member of the House of Representatives (above) during the Crédit Mobilier scandal and the "salary grab."

gressmen at a big discount. In exchange, they voted to give huge loans, land grants, and building contracts to Crédit Mobilier. The scandal hit the news in 1872. James, always on the lookout for money-making schemes, had bought some shares. Although he was cleared of wrongdoing, the affair cast a shadow on his name.

Another scandal was the "salary grab." In 1873, Congress voted huge salary increases for government offi-cials. Congressmen's salaries went up 50 percent, from $5,000 to $7,500. The president's salary doubled—from $25,000 to $50,000. Americans were so outraged that most of the raises were cut out the next year. James had opposed the raises, but they were just a small part of a very large budget. As chairman of the Appropriations Com-mittee, he was under pressure to approve the whole package. But to the public, this made him look greedy and self-serving.

Nothing New: Scandals Plague Presidency

✯ ✯ ✯ ✯ ✯ ✯ ✯ ✯ ✯ ✯ ✯ ✯ ✯ ✯ ✯ ✯ ✯ ✯ ✯

James Garfield was not the first, nor will he be the last president to suffer from scandal, real or imagined. Political adversaries would not let Andrew Jackson, the seventh president, forget that he had (unknowingly) married Rachel Donelson Robards before her first marriage had legally ended. Abraham Lincoln's opponents maintained that Mary Todd Lincoln was a Confederate spy because of her Southern family. In the 1920s, Warren Harding's administration was plagued by the Teapot Dome Scandal. The president had made his friend Albert Fall secretary of the interior, but Mr. Fall was more interested in the interior of his wallet than that of the country. He leased oil-rich federal reserve land to oil companies at low cost, accepting "loans" in return. Richard Nixon's presidency ended abruptly when it was established that he helped cover up the burglary of the Democratic National Committee's headquarters in the Watergate scandal. The Iran-Contra Affair broke in the summer of 1987, during Ronald Reagan's presidency. Members of the Reagan administration conspired to fund rebel Contras—behind the back of Congress—in the Central American country of Nicaragua with money earned from selling weapons to Iran. During the Bush administration, it surfaced that members of Congress were using their free mail privilege for personal as well as official mail. A recent Washington upheaval concerned illegal funds for the Clinton-Gore 1996 re-election campaign coming from foreign contributors.

James was also caught up in the Republican Party's fights. Republicans were split between the Stalwarts and the Half-Breeds.

Ulysses S. Grant, president from 1869 to 1877, was a Stalwart. He believed in the "spoils system." This meant that he gave government jobs to political friends instead of to people who had earned them. For instance, he let his Stalwart ally, New York senator Roscoe Conkling, hand out

Ulysses S. Grant

Roscoe Conkling

Rutherford B. Hayes

Edward "Ned" Garfield

all the federal jobs in the very large state of New York.

Rutherford B. Hayes, the next president, was against the spoils system. Stalwarts called him a Half-Breed, or half-hearted Republican. When Hayes took away Conkling's privileges, Stalwarts hated him. Because James was on Hayes's side, he, too, made plenty of enemies.

James and Lucretia kept in touch constantly. He discussed government business with her, shared his problems, and asked her advice. Both were brokenhearted when little Ned died of whooping cough at the age of two.

The Garfields' home in Mentor, Ohio, was later named Lawnfield.

(This was another childhood disease that is easily treated today.) They laid him to rest in Hiram Cemetery, next to their daughter Eliza's grave.

The Garfields still needed a summer home. One day in the fall of 1876, James bought a farm near Mentor, Ohio. It needed a lot of work. According to one visitor, "The shaky old barns stood amid heaps of rubbish. . . . The pig sty wafted its sweetness . . . to the windows of the parlor." But at least it was a home. James wrote to Lucretia, "So my darling, you shall have a home and a cow."

In the spring, Lucretia flew into

James and Lucretia with Mollie and James's mother

55

Croquet, Anyone?

★ ★

The first outdoor game concocted for play by men and women together, croquet was all the rage in the late 1800s. A course of two poles and numerous wire hoops

(called wickets) was set up on a flat lawn, and players took turns knocking softball-sized balls through the hoops with mallets. Since no running or jumping was required, croquet became most popular among women and older people looking for outdoor recreation that strained neither their corseted, full-skirted fashions nor their elderly hearts. Young romantics often found croquet convenient for spending unchaperoned time with their sweethearts. Girls were advised to strike stunning poses while they played. Competitors often played into the evening, setting candles atop their wickets. Originally from France, the game became so popular in England that the championships were held at Wimbledon, today most associated with the best in tennis.

the frenzy of fixing up their new home. She and James attacked everything at once. The farmhouse was only one-and-a-half stories high. Paint was peeling, rooms were small, and ceilings were low. Carpenters repaired the house while Lucretia made it livable. She bought new furniture, kitchen crockery, and supplies. Mollie, now ten years old, was her best little helper.

James bought horses and plowed fields. Harry and Jim, now big boys and full of energy, pitched in, too.

The Garfields enjoyed spending time at Lawnfield with their family and friends.

They planted barley, corn, hay, and fruit trees. Irvin and Abe, ages six and four, tumbled around in the haystacks. As he had promised, James bought Lucretia a cow.

The children loved roaming around the 160-acre (65-ha) farm. They swam, fished, rode horses, and played croquet. One of their favorite games was puss-in-the-corner, and their parents even joined in sometimes. Here is how it went. Four people stood in the corners of a room or in four spots outdoors. Then they ran to switch corners. A fifth person, in the middle, tried to race to a corner while it was empty.

For the next few years, the Garfields were more interested in the farm than almost anything else. By the spring of 1880, the farmhouse was big, roomy, and comfortable. Lucretia had never worked so hard before, yet she had never felt so good. She and James were apart sometimes for weeks at a time, but they had become close companions. When they were together, they made the most of their time. They read books, went visiting, and took trips whenever they could.

By 1880, James had served in the House of Representatives for seventeen years. He decided to run for the U.S. Senate and won. However, he

The Republicans argued mightily over the presidential nomination during the 1880 national convention in Chicago.

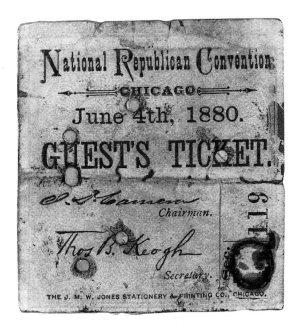

A guest's ticket to the 1880 Republican National Convention

did not have much time to serve. He was chosen to be a delegate to the Republican National Convention in Chicago in June 1880.

Several men had stepped forward hoping to be the Republican candidate for president. Ulysses S. Grant, James Blaine, and Ohioan John Sherman were the front-runners. James strongly supported Sherman and made the speech to nominate him.

Hour after hour, day after day, the delegates argued and fought. Stalwarts and Half-Breeds were furious with each other. James wrote to

The National Woman Suffrage Association conducted a membership meeting at the convention.

Lucretia, "You can never know how much I need you during these days of storm. . . . When I am safely with you again my joy will be full."

On Monday, June 7, delegates began voting. Whoever received a majority vote would be the presidential candidate. Grant got the most votes, but no one had received more than half. A second vote was taken, and a third. By the thirty-third ballot, there was still no winner.

Some delegates began to call for Garfield himself. But James grumbled and groused. He insisted he was there to push for Sherman and nothing else.

Metal campaign badges like this one were worn by supporters of James Garfield.

A campaign poster for James A. Garfield and his running mate, Chester A. Arthur

This political cartoon shows Garfield as the "Friend of the Freeman."

Lucretia's opinion was firm: "I don't want you to have the nomination merely because no one else can get it. I want you to have it when the whole country calls for you. . . . My ambition does not stop short of that."

On the thirty-fourth ballot, Wisconsin delegates voted "Garfield!" This let loose what reporters called a "stampede." One by one, delegates who hated Grant switched their votes to James. On the thirty-sixth ballot, he won the nomination.

James Garfield poses with friends on the porch of Lawnfield during the summer of 1880.

Garfield's "consultation office" at Lawnfield was a very busy place during the campaign of 1880.

Crowds of supporters visited James at Lawnfield during the summer and fall of 1880.

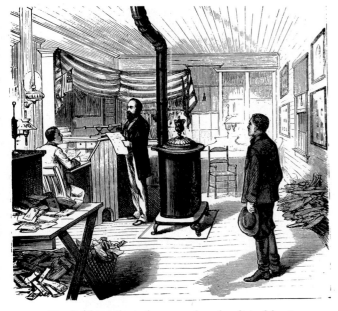

Garfield conducted personal and political business in this office at Lawnfield.

The Democratic candidate was General Winfield Scott Hancock, a hero of the Civil War battle of Gettysburg. James took a few trips to make campaign speeches. For most of the summer, though, he and Lucretia worked the farm and tried to relax. But an endless stream of well-wishers found their way to the Garfields' farmhouse door.

Visitors included 95 ladies and gentlemen from Indiana, 400 members of a Garfield fan club, 1,000 Cleveland businessmen, and even 7 railroad cars loaded with Germans. One day, more than 5,000 people appeared in the pouring rain. James delivered speeches from the front porch and gave tours of the farm, which reporters were now calling Lawnfield. Lucretia served coffee, snacks, lunches, and dinners. Some guests even stayed overnight.

By election time in November, James and Lucretia were exhausted, but their efforts paid off. James was elected twentieth president of the United States.

★ ★ ★ ★ ★ ★ ★ ★ ★ ★ ★ ★ ★ ★ ★

CHAPTER SIX

First Lady—For a While

☆ ☆ ☆ ☆ ☆ ☆ ☆ ☆ ☆ ☆ ☆ ☆ ☆ ☆ ☆

Lucretia was about to become First Lady of the United States. It was time for some serious shopping! In January 1881, with the inauguration only two months away, she went to New York City to visit dressmakers. To escape prying reporters, she used the name "Mrs. Greenfield."

Meanwhile, James was picking his presidential advisors. He tried to choose people who shared his views, without making Conkling's Stalwarts too angry. Chester A. Arthur, a Stalwart, would be vice president. But James chose anti-Stalwarts for other important jobs. Republicans on all sides hounded him daily.

☆ ☆ ☆ ☆ ☆ ☆ ☆ ☆ ☆ ☆ ☆ ☆ ☆ ☆ ☆

President Garfield at the White House in a meeting with his cabinet

It seemed that no one was happy, neither Stalwarts nor anti-Stalwarts.

On Inauguration Day, March 4, Lucretia was jolted awake at 3:00 in the morning. Outside was a raging storm. Rain, sleet, and snow pelted the windowpanes. As for James, he had only finished writing his inaugural speech at 2:30 A.M. The two exhausted Garfields had a long day ahead of them.

Luckily, the skies cleared in time for the ceremonies. Together, James and Lucretia took their place on a platform in front of the Capitol. "The vast concourse of people . . . covering all the vast space in front of the Capitol was the grandest human spec-

Choosing the Vice President

★ ★

Today, it seems strange that James Garfield would be paired with Chester Alan Arthur, a Stalwart of different views, as his vice-presidential running mate. In modern politics, a party's presidential nominee selects his or her vice-presidential candidate, and the two usually agree on the issues. This was not always the case. At first, electors (a group of prominent men in each state chosen by the legislature) voted for two people for president. The person with the most votes became president, and the runner-up became vice president. After the passage of the Twelfth Amendment to the Constitution in 1804, electors cast two separate ballots, one for president and one for vice president. By 1828, the voters finally got into the act when it became their job to elect the electors. The people voted for the elector they knew would cast his ballots for their candidates. When national party conventions began in 1831, each party nominated two candidates with differing views to create a "balanced ticket" that would appeal to the widest number of voters. (The vice-presidential slot was also a "consolation" prize for that faction of the party whose man lost the presidential nomination.) That is why the Republican National Convention chose Arthur to run with Garfield. This system faded, however, because if the president died in office (as did Garfield), a vice president with different opinions would take his place. By World War II, presidential candidates selected their own running mates.

President Garfield

Vice President Arthur

67

James Garfield took the oath of office as president on March 4, 1881.

Lucy Hayes

tacle I have ever seen," the proud First Lady wrote.

Lucy Hayes, the outgoing First Lady, served them lunch. It was her last official duty in the White House. Lucretia liked Lucy. They were the first two First Ladies to have earned college degrees. She waved as the Hayeses drove off in a carriage, leaving the White House to the Garfields.

At 9:00 that evening, the inaugural reception began. It was the first event ever held at the Smithsonian Institution's new National Museum building. When the dancing began at 11:00, the weary Garfields went home.

James Garfield's inaugural reception was held at the Smithsonian Institution.

Having a Ball in America's Attic

✫ ✫ ✫ ✫ ✫ ✫ ✫ ✫ ✫ ✫ ✫ ✫ ✫ ✫ ✫ ✫ ✫ ✫ ✫ ✫

As guests at James Garfield's Inaugural Ball danced the night away, little did they realize that the lovely new building they were enjoying would one day be a part of the largest museum complex in the world. The Smithsonian Institution had been the gift of an Englishman named James Smithson whose will bequeathed money to the United States to construct "an Establishment for the increase and diffusion of knowledge. . . ." For many years, the money was used for research, until finally the Smithsonian undertook its mission as a museum. The first building to be completed was the Castle, a delightful storybook creation topped with spires and turrets. It remains today the symbol of the Smithsonian. The National Museum was completed in time for the Garfield inaugural festivities in 1881. It was built to house more than sixty railroad carloads of exhibits from Philadelphia's huge 1876 world's fair. Today called the Arts and Industries Building, it has been beautifully restored to its original appearance. Since the National Museum was built, the Smithsonian has added twelve more museums in Washington, D.C., and one in New York City. The Smithsonian's collections include about 137 million objects, and its exhibits cover everything from fine art to space exploration to the gowns of America's First Ladies. Often called the "nation's attic," the Smithsonian Institution is indeed a rare treasure.

When James became president, the Garfield family included (left to right, standing) Harry, Mollie, Jim, (left to right, seated) Abram, Lucretia, James, Irvin, and James's mother, Eliza, called Mother Garfield.

After the ceremonies, the Garfield family settled into their new home. With Harry and Jim away at school, that left thirteen-year-old Mollie, ten-year-old Irvin, and eight-year-old Abram. The children had a great time in the White House. "My boys," Lucretia said, "go tumbling through it with their handsprings and somersaults." One day, "Mollie had 10 little girls to lunch." Everyone was excited about living in the great mansion for the next four years.

Lucretia was swept into a whirlwind of official duties. There were formal receptions and dinners with diplomats, military officers, congressmen, and their wives. Lucretia held her own receptions in the White House on Tuesdays and Fridays. James was proud of his gracious and charming wife. He had never seen this side

A view of the White House as it looked in 1881, when James Garfield became president

of her before. Overnight, she had blossomed into a perfect hostess.

Reporters asked Lucretia for details about her life. They wanted to give the hungry public some delicious news about the First Lady. But she replied, "I have done nothing that can be written about. Wait until I have, and then

This gown, worn by Lucretia when she was First Lady, can be seen at the Smithsonian.

it will be time enough to write." Photographers begged to take the First Lady's picture. Lucretia, however, usually declined. She said she was only Mr. Garfield's companion.

In the daytime, hordes of pesky office-seekers came to the White House asking James for jobs. He began to think that something needed to be done about the federal job system.

One thing about life in the White House annoyed Lucretia. Old friends thought they could make themselves at home there, just as they had at the farmhouse. Some simply showed up and camped out. They would wander around until they found a comfortable sofa, then curl up for a nice, cozy nap.

Lucretia fretted about "the dilapidated condition of this old White House" and decided to redecorate. She spent hours in the Library of Congress, studying the history of the White House and its furnishings. On a trip to New York, she shopped for carpets for the parlors.

One evening in early May, several people were gathered in the White House for a social evening. Lucretia was feeling chilly and huddled by the

First Lady Lucretia Rudolph Garfield

fireplace to chat with her guests. The next day, she was shaking with chills. Her fever shot up to 104 degrees Fahrenheit (40 degrees Celsius). One doctor decided that she was suffering from "nervous prostration." This simply meant that she was worn out. James, unhappy with the diagnosis,

73

In Garfield's day, as now, Washington, D.C., was a popular tourist destination.

called in another doctor, who declared that Lucretia had malaria.

Malaria was a common disease in the 1800s. People thought it was caused by bad vapors in the air. In fact, the word "malaria" comes from the Italian words *mal aria*, meaning "bad air." It began with headaches, aching joints, and low energy. Next, fever and violent chills set in. One of every ten people with malaria died. Only a year before Lucretia got sick, a French doctor discovered that a certain mosquito

Lucretia Garfield leaving the White House for an evening ride

FRANCKLYN COTTAGE.

James took Lucretia to Elberon, New Jersey, hoping the ocean air might help her regain her health after a bout with malaria.

spread the disease. It would be years, though, before doctors accepted this.

James dropped most of his official business to care for his wife. "I refuse to see people on business," he wrote; "all my thoughts center in her, in comparison with whom all else fades into insignificance."

Lucretia's weakness and fever continued through the month of May. James doted and fussed over her. Day after day, he noted her condition in his diary. "The dear one slept better last night," he wrote, and "The precious one is better again."

At last the fever passed. Greatly relieved, James and the children traveled with Lucretia to Elberon, New Jersey. James believed that the air in this oceanside town would help her regain her strength. At the end of June, James returned to Washington.

James Garfield, on his way to a Williams College reunion, was shot in a Washington, D.C., train station on the morning of July 2, 1881.

Lucretia stayed in Elberon, feeling stronger every day.

July 3, 1881, was to be the twenty-fifth anniversary of James's graduation from Williams College. He was looking forward to visiting his old school again for the reunion. At the same time, he planned to enroll Harry and Jim in the freshman class.

On the morning of July 2, James left the White House to catch a train to Williamstown. At 9:20 A.M., he entered the station. Just then, a crazed man with a .44-caliber revolver stepped forward and fired. James took bullets in the arm and the back and collapsed to the floor. Bystanders grabbed the shooter and wrestled him to the ground, while others carried James into an office.

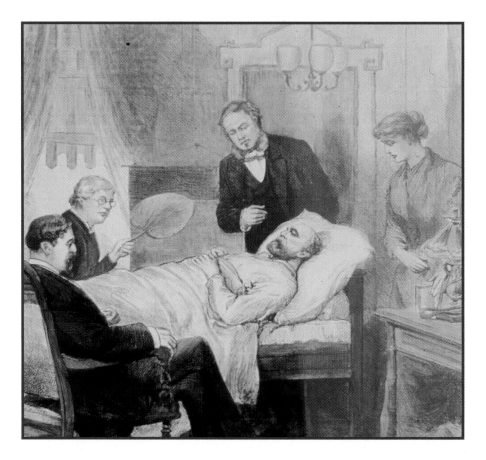

Lucretia rushed from Elberon to James's bedside in the White House as soon as she heard the news that he had been shot.

Minutes later, Harry and Jim walked into a station that was wild with chaos. Nevertheless, they kept their heads and helped get their father back to the White House. Lucretia was quickly notified. Doctors told James that he was bleeding internally and that his chances were not good. But he was more concerned about Lucretia than he was about himself.

He was worried that the news might make her condition worse.

At noon the next day, Lucretia and Mollie boarded a train for Washington. It was close to 7:00 P.M. when they finally reached the White House. Lucretia rushed directly to James's bedside and spent a long time alone with him.

Eventually he said, "Go now and

Her Bedside Manner

✶ ✶

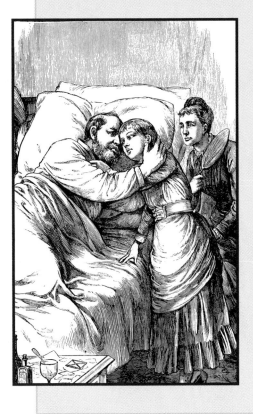

Lucretia's bravery during her husband's ordeal became legendary. In 1881, James's biographer described her courageous manner in flowery nineteenth-century language: "She never left him in all those weary days of pain, and she it was who, on many occasions, brought him back to consciousness and life by tender care, when it seemed to others that the slender thread which bound him to earth was too weak longer to hold. . . . Even the medical attendants were unanimous in according her the first praise for attentions which were more important to the patient than any they could render. . . . This toil was constant, day by day, without intermission, except a few hours for sleep, and to the exclusion of all thoughts for her own health or comfort, she may well be cited as one of the noblest examples of true wifehood in any age or country."

rest; I shall want you near me when the crisis comes." At the time, she refused to believe that he was talking about his own death. Observers noted that she was calm and composed when she left his room.

The hot, muggy summer days passed. A corner room of the White House was set up as James's sickroom. Air conditioning would not be invented for another forty years. However, Navy engineers rigged up a refrigerating machine that kept the room cool and dry.

Lucretia often fixed meals for James in the White House kitchen.

Charles J. Guiteau, who shot James Garfield, stood trial for his crime.

Lucretia visited him every morning and usually again later in the day. Meanwhile, the gunman, Charles J. Guiteau, sat in prison awaiting his trial. Why did he do it?

After firing at Garfield, Guiteau had declared, "I did it and I want to go to jail! I am a Stalwart and Arthur is president now!" Investigators found out that Guiteau had visited the White House many times hoping to get a job. His idea was that he should be minister to Austria or consul general to Paris. He became so bothersome

While James fought for his life inside the White House, soldiers camped on the lawn outside to wait for the latest news.

Crowds gathered around this bulletin board in Richmond, Virginia, to read the news of the assassination attempt.

that the White House doorman had stopped letting him in.

As a staunch Stalwart, Guiteau was angry that Garfield had not given any political favors to Roscoe Conkling. Guiteau believed that he, too, was snubbed because he was a Stalwart. To him, getting rid of Garfield would fix these injustices in the Republican Party. He had stalked James for weeks, looking for his chance to kill. Guiteau, found guilty of murder, was hanged on June 30, 1882.

Throughout the summer, Lucretia was weak from her bout with malaria. Still, she tried to stay calm and keep up the usual routine of life in the White House. "The wife of the president is the bravest woman in the universe," one of the doctors said.

News from the White House shot around the country like a speeding bullet. By this time, reporters could send stories to faraway cities by telegraph. Across the land, people felt as if they were at James's bedside, right along with Lucretia and the children. In their rush to outdo one another, many reporters made up stories. The *New York Tribune* commented, "Sick-

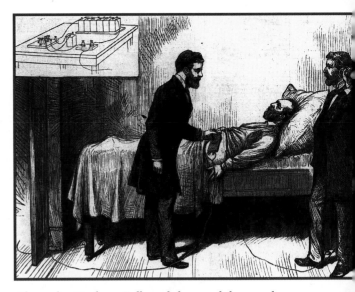

Alexander Graham Bell used the metal detector he had invented to try to find the bullet.

room scenes which never had any existence have been described in feverish rhetoric."

One bullet was lodged deep in James's back, but no one knew just where it was. Surgery to find it would be too risky, so the doctors poked and probed with dirty fingers and instruments. Unfortunately, Dr. Walter Cannon, the first to use medical X rays, was only ten years old at the time!

The doctors called in Alexander Graham Bell, who had just invented the telephone. Bell had also invented

81

Alexander Graham Bell (1847–1922)

★ ★

It really is no wonder that Alexander Graham Bell invented the telephone. He came from a family of "phoneticists"—people who study the sounds of speech. He used his father's invention of "Visible Speech," an alphabet of signs standing for actual sounds, to teach deaf children to speak. So, when it came to transmitting speech over wires with electricity, Alexander knew more about speech than just about anyone. What's amazing is that he figured out how to make the telephone work after part of another invention, the multiple telegraph, got stuck. Bell shouted to his assistant Thomas Watson in the next room to twang the stuck piece free. When Watson did so, Bell saw the receiver in his room vibrate all by itself. This observation led to his idea for the telephone in 1875.

a kind of metal detector, which he used to try to find the bullet. This method did not work very well. Bell thought that the bullet might be on James's right side. But he could not be sure, because every time he used the detector, the metal bedsprings set off signals, too. In reality, the bullet was on the left.

In August, James developed a bad infection and a high fever. He wanted to get out of Washington, so he was taken by train on a cot to Elberon, New Jersey. Lucretia sat by his bedside

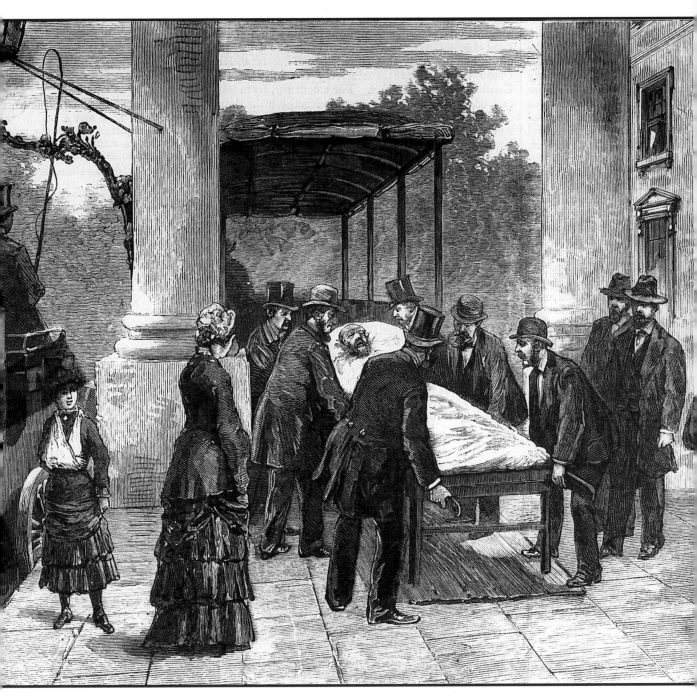

President Garfield was put on a cot and removed from his sickbed at the White House so he could be taken to Elberon, New Jersey.

The Journey to Elberon

✳ ✳

About sixty days into his ordeal, James was transferred to a seaside cottage at Elberon, New Jersey. To ease his journey, workers constructed a special rail line as described by Garfield's biographer in 1881: "Down at Elberon there is a weird scene tonight. Three hundred skilled engineers and workmen—a loyal company of sturdy patriots—are laying a temporary track to connect the main line with the cottages on the beach. . . . The length of the new track is 3,200 feet [975 m]. It is to be laid directly to the hotel grounds, describing a curve to the very door of Francklyn cottage. . . ." Railroad men were ordered "to stop every freight and passenger train that might be on the road between Baltimore and Washington on half an hour's notice, and to give the special train the right of way at any hour of the day or night." This not only gave the ill president's train a clear road to travel, but prevented other trains from passing the special so that the president would not be bothered by jostling or noise.

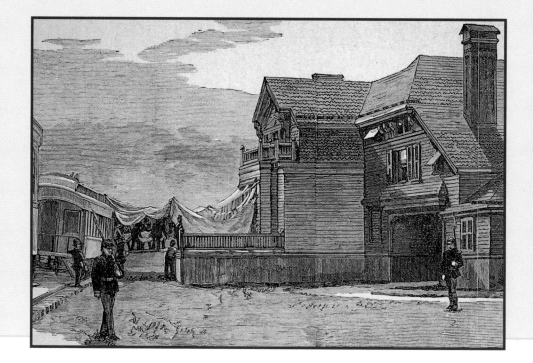

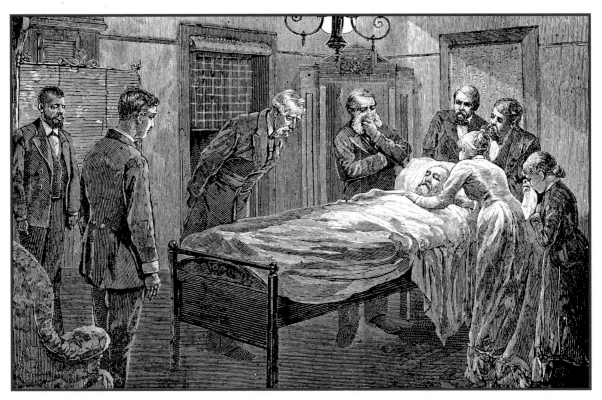

James Garfield died on the night of September 19, 1881, about two-and-a-half months after he had been shot by Charles Guiteau.

reading letters, telegrams, and newspaper articles. The two often had a good laugh over some of the dramatic stories written about him.

On the night of September 19, James grabbed his chest and cried, "How it hurts here!" A nurse ran to get Lucretia and the doctor. Lucretia could tell that this was the end. According to the doctor, she exclaimed, "Oh why am I made to suffer this cruel wrong?" Then she took her husband's hand and held it quietly. At 10:35 P.M., James's heart stopped beating. He had died.

Lucretia ran to her room, collapsed, and cried bitterly. Soon, she emerged and went back to James's deathbed. There, she simply sat alone beside her husband of twenty-three years.

Vacationing with the Presidents

✯ ✯

The seaside community where James Garfield died of his wounds was usually a happier place. Located on the Atlantic Ocean in northern New Jersey, Long Branch (of which Elberon is a part) first became popular as a resort after Ulysses S. Grant began vacationing there in 1869. He would spend every summer of his presidency there and more. That presidential endorsement was enough to make Long Branch the nation's most popular summer resort. A racetrack, beachside boardwalk, and gambling casinos added to the attractions of fresh sea air and pounding surf. Shady characters, actors, politicians, and society women rubbed elbows there, and Long Branch's more racy aspects prompted one observer to note that it was not a place where a responsible parent would take the family for a quiet summer by the sea. Nonetheless, Long Branch became the haunt of no fewer than seven presidents at one time or another. Today, they are remembered at the Church of the Presidents and at Seven Presidents Oceanfront Park. At Garfield Terrace, a monument marks the location of Francklyn cottage, the house where President Garfield died.

Messages of sympathy began pouring in the next day. James, two months short of his fiftieth birthday, was the fourth U.S. president to die in office. William Henry Harrison and Zachary Taylor had died of illnesses. Abraham Lincoln, like Garfield, had been the victim of an assassin's bullet.

James's body was brought back to Washington to lie in state in the Capitol. After the funeral, his casket was put on a train to Cleveland. All along the route, throngs of mourners lined the tracks. An estimated 250,000 people crowded into Cleveland for his public memorial. Unlike previous widowed First Ladies, Lucretia attended her husband's funeral. He was buried in Cleveland's Lake View Cemetery.

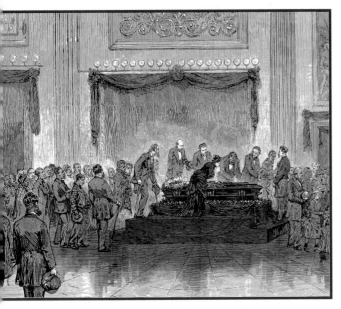

President Garfield's coffin lies in state in the Capitol Rotunda.

About 250,000 people crowded into Cleveland for Garfield's public memorial.

Garfield's funeral train passes through Princeton on its way from Washington to Cleveland.

CHAPTER SEVEN

"Faultless Taste"

* * * * * * * * * * * * * * * *

After the funeral, Lucretia and the children settled in Cleveland. There would be no more winters in Washington, D.C. Those days were gone forever. Lucretia's reign as First Lady had lasted only six months. She would never get to finish redecorating the White House. In time, she returned to her beloved Lawnfield farm. The big, rambling house seemed empty now, without James's dynamic presence.

Lucretia took on one last project at the farm. She added nine new rooms to the farmhouse, including a library. There she gathered together all the letters and documents from James's long career in public life. This

* * * * * * * * * * * * * * * *

After Lucretia returned to the Lawnfield farm, she added nine new rooms to the already large house. One of the rooms was a library to house all the letters, documents, and memorabilia from James's political career.

was to be the first memorial library for a U.S. president. In time, the papers—as well as Lucretia's own letters and diaries—were donated to the Library of Congress.

Americans were so moved by Lucretia's tragedy that they raised a fund for her. Through private donations, it grew to over $360,000. In today's terms, that would be equal to about six million dollars!

Another First Lady helped Lucretia to be free of money worries—Julia Tyler, widow of tenth president John Tyler. Julia worked hard to persuade Congress to grant a pension to presidents' widows. In March 1882, Congress approved a pension of $5,000 a year. It benefitted four widowed First Ladies who were still living at the time—Julia, Lucretia, Mary Lincoln, and Sarah Polk.

This picture of Lucretia with her children was taken thirty years after James's death. Left to right, Irvin, Mollie, Abram, Lucretia, James, and Harry.

Lucretia watched her children grow to become happy, successful adults. Mollie married Joseph Stanley-Brown, who had been her father's secretary. Eventually, they settled in Pasadena, California. Lucretia spent the cold winter months in sunny California, too. She built a beautiful home for herself in Pasadena. When summer rolled around, though, she always returned to Lawnfield.

Harry, Jim, and Irvin became lawyers. Harry became president of Williams College, and Jim served as U.S. secretary of the interior under President Theodore Roosevelt. Abram became an architect. In 1961, Jim's grandson Newell married Jane Harrison Walker, the granddaughter of the twenty-third president, Benjamin Harrison.

After Garfield's assassination, Americans realized that they needed to reform the way government jobs were given out. In 1883, Congress passed the Pendleton Federal Civil

The tombs of James and Lucretia are housed inside the Garfield Monument in Lake View Cemetery.

Service Act. This set up the Civil Service Commission to put federal jobs on the merit system.

Lucretia lived for almost thirty-seven years after James's death. When she left the farm in the fall of 1917, she would never see it again. On March 14, 1918, in Pasadena, California, she died. She would have been eighty-six years old in April. In Cleveland's Lake View Cemetery, a fabulous monument had been built for James's tomb. Lucretia was placed next to him, in a spot that had been waiting for her all those years.

Today, Lucretia Garfield has dozens of great-great-great-grandchildren all over the United States. Many are schoolchildren who are studying right now about the history of their country. They can be especially proud of Lucretia, a lady of courage, intelligence, and faith. She may have had more than her share of troubles, but, as James once wrote, Lucretia "grows up to every new emergency with fine tact and faultless taste."

Portrait of America, 1918: The War to End All Wars

✫ ✫

By the year Lucretia died, America had all its states except Alaska and Hawaii, and for the first time, more Americans lived in cities than anywhere else. The population numbered 103 million, and it is likely that all of them were talking about the First World War. Of course, no one called it that because everyone believed that this horrible war would be the last ever. The Great War they called it, and it had raged in Europe since 1914. America sent troops to fight in 1917. By the time it ended on November 11, 1918, well over 100,000 Americans had died. President Woodrow Wilson left for Paris in December to attend the peace conference.

Despite the happy news of the war's end, 1918 must have been a difficult year. As if the war weren't enough, a worldwide influenza epidemic at the same time took 500,000 lives in the United States and 20 million around the globe. Half the American soldiers who perished in Europe died of disease. Besides war and disease, Americans suffered through coal, oil, and gasoline rationing. They voluntarily observed "meatless" and "wheatless" days to help the war effort. In March, the government enacted daylight savings time to conserve energy. Grim though life was, patriotic Americans rolled up their sleeves and did their part. They knitted socks and hats for the soldiers and donated books for them to read. As the men went off to war, women took their jobs to keep the economy rolling.

And, in spite of the war, 1918 saw the fifteenth World Series, in which a young Babe Ruth pitched the Boston Red Sox to a 4-to-2 victory over Chicago.

✫ ✫ ✫ ✫ ✫ ✫ ✫ ✫ ✫ ✫ ✫ ✫ ✫ ✫ ✫

The Presidents and Their First Ladies

President	Birth–Death	First Lady	Birth–Death
1789–1797			
George Washington	1732–1799	Martha Dandridge Custis Washington	1731–1802
1797–1801			
John Adams	1735–1826	Abigail Smith Adams	1744–1818
1801–1809			
Thomas Jefferson†	1743–1826		
1809–1817			
James Madison	1751–1836	Dolley Payne Todd Madison	1768–1849
1817–1825			
James Monroe	1758–1831	Elizabeth Kortright Monroe	1768–1830
1825–1829			
John Quincy Adams	1767–1848	Louisa Catherine Johnson Adams	1775–1852
1829–1837			
Andrew Jackson†	1767–1845		
1837–1841			
Martin Van Buren†	1782–1862		
1841			
William Henry Harrison‡	1773–1841		
1841–1845			
John Tyler	1790–1862	Letitia Christian Tyler (1841–1842)	1790–1842
		Julia Gardiner Tyler (1844–1845)	1820–1889
1845–1849			
James K. Polk	1795–1849	Sarah Childress Polk	1803–1891
1849–1850			
Zachary Taylor	1784–1850	Margaret Mackall Smith Taylor	1788–1852
1850–1853			
Millard Fillmore	1800–1874	Abigail Powers Fillmore	1798–1853
1853–1857			
Franklin Pierce	1804–1869	Jane Means Appleton Pierce	1806–1863
1857–1861			
James Buchanan*	1791–1868		
1861–1865			
Abraham Lincoln	1809–1865	Mary Todd Lincoln	1818–1882
1865–1869			
Andrew Johnson	1808–1875	Eliza McCardle Johnson	1810–1876
1869–1877			
Ulysses S. Grant	1822–1885	Julia Dent Grant	1826–1902
1877–1881			
Rutherford B. Hayes	1822–1893	Lucy Ware Webb Hayes	1831–1889
1881			
James A. Garfield	1831–1881	Lucretia Rudolph Garfield	1832–1918
1881–1885			
Chester A. Arthur†	1829–1886		

† wife died before he took office   ‡ wife too ill to accompany him to Washington   * never married

1885–1889			
Grover Cleveland	1837–1908	Frances Folsom Cleveland	1864–1947
1889–1893			
Benjamin Harrison	1833–1901	Caroline Lavinia Scott Harrison	1832–1892
1893–1897			
Grover Cleveland	1837–1908	Frances Folsom Cleveland	1864–1947
1897–1901			
William McKinley	1843–1901	Ida Saxton McKinley	1847–1907
1901–1909			
Theodore Roosevelt	1858–1919	Edith Kermit Carow Roosevelt	1861–1948
1909–1913			
William Howard Taft	1857–1930	Helen Herron Taft	1861–1943
1913–1921			
Woodrow Wilson	1856–1924	Ellen Louise Axson Wilson (1913–1914)	1860–1914
		Edith Bolling Galt Wilson (1915–1921)	1872–1961
1921–1923			
Warren G. Harding	1865–1923	Florence Kling Harding	1860–1924
1923–1929			
Calvin Coolidge	1872–1933	Grace Anna Goodhue Coolidge	1879–1957
1929–1933			
Herbert Hoover	1874–1964	Lou Henry Hoover	1874–1944
1933–1945			
Franklin D. Roosevelt	1882–1945	Anna Eleanor Roosevelt	1884–1962
1945–1953			
Harry S. Truman	1884–1972	Bess Wallace Truman	1885–1982
1953–1961			
Dwight D. Eisenhower	1890–1969	Mamie Geneva Doud Eisenhower	1896–1979
1961–1963			
John F. Kennedy	1917–1963	Jacqueline Bouvier Kennedy	1929–1994
1963–1969			
Lyndon B. Johnson	1908–1973	Claudia Taylor (Lady Bird) Johnson	1912–
1969–1974			
Richard Nixon	1913–1994	Patricia Ryan Nixon	1912–1993
1974–1977			
Gerald Ford	1913–	Elizabeth Bloomer Ford	1918–
1977–1981			
James Carter	1924–	Rosalynn Smith Carter	1927–
1981–1989			
Ronald Reagan	1911–	Nancy Davis Reagan	1923–
1989–1993			
George Bush	1924–	Barbara Pierce Bush	1925–
1993–			
William Jefferson Clinton	1946–	Hillary Rodham Clinton	1947–

Lucretia Rudolph Garfield Timeline

1831 ★ James A. Garfield is born

William Lloyd Garrison publishes *The Liberator*, an antislavery newspaper

1832 ★ Andrew Jackson is reelected president

New England Anti-Slavery Society is founded in Boston, Massachusetts

Lucretia Rudolph is born

1833 ★ Oberlin College becomes the first college to admit women

1836 ★ Martin Van Buren is elected president

Texas declares independence from Mexico

Mexican army defeats Texans at the Alamo

1837 ★ Economic depression spreads throughout the United States

1838 ★ Native Americans are forced from the southeastern United States to present-day Oklahoma; many die along the Trail of Tears

1840 ★ William Henry Harrison is elected president

1841 ★ William Henry Harrison dies a month after taking office and John Tyler becomes president

1844 ★ James K. Polk is elected president

1845 ★ U.S. Naval Academy opens at Annapolis, Maryland

1846 ★ United States declares war on Mexico

United States annexes New Mexico from Mexico

Oregon Territory is divided between United States and Great Britain at the 49th parallel

1847 ★ Maria Mitchell is the first woman elected to the American Academy of Arts and Sciences

Smithsonian Institution is formally dedicated

1848	★	Treaty of Guadalupe Hidalgo ends the Mexican War and gives most of the present-day Southwest to the United States
		First U.S. women's rights meeting is held in Seneca Falls, New York
		Gold is discovered in California
		Zachary Taylor is elected president
1849	★	Elizabeth Blackwell becomes the first woman in the world to receive a medical degree
		California gold rush starts
1850	★	Zachary Taylor dies and Millard Fillmore becomes president
		Compromise of 1850 admits California as a free state
		Lucretia Rudolph graduates from Geauga Seminary
1852	★	Franklin Pierce is elected president
1853	★	United States acquires the rest of the present-day Southwest through the Gadsden Purchase
1854	★	Republican Party is formed
		Kansas-Nebraska Act allows the two territories to decide for themselves whether or not to allow slavery
		Lucretia Rudolph graduates from the Eclectic
1856	★	James Buchanan is elected president
1858	★	Lucretia Rudolph marries James A. Garfield
1860	★	James A. Garfield wins a seat in the Ohio State Senate
		Elizabeth Arabella Garfield is born
		Abraham Lincoln is elected president
1861	★	Confederate States of America (eleven seceded Southern states) is formed
		Confederates fire on Fort Sumter, starting the Civil War
		James A. Garfield joins the Union army
1862	★	Confederate army defeats Union forces at the Second Battle of Bull Run and at Fredericksburg
		James A. Garfield is elected to the U.S. House of Representatives

1863	★	President Lincoln issues the Emancipation Proclamation
		James A. Garfield fights in the Battle of Chickamauga and becomes a major general
		Union forces defeat the Confederacy in major battles at Gettysburg and Vicksburg
		Harry Augustus Garfield is born
		President Lincoln gives the Gettysburg Address
		Elizabeth Arabella Garfield dies
1864	★	Lucretia Garfield moves to Washington, D.C.
		Abraham Lincoln is reelected president
1865	★	Confederate general Robert E. Lee surrenders to Union general Ulysses S. Grant at Appomattox Courthouse
		Abraham Lincoln is assassinated
		Andrew Johnson becomes president
		James Rudolph Garfield is born
1867	★	United States purchases the Alaska territory from Russia
		Mary "Mollie" Garfield is born
1868	★	Ulysses S. Grant is elected president
1870	★	Irvin Garfield is born
1871	★	Chicago fire destroys most of that city
1872	★	Abram Garfield is born
		Ulysses S. Grant is reelected president
		Yellowstone National Park is established
1874	★	Edward "Ned" Garfield is born
1876	★	General George Armstrong Custer and his troops are killed at the Battle of the Little Big Horn
		Alexander Graham Bell patents the telephone
		Edward "Ned" Garfield dies
1877	★	Rutherford Hayes becomes president
1880	★	In January, James A. Garfield is selected to represent Ohio in the U.S. Senate
		In November, Garfield is elected president

1881	★	James A . Garfield is shot and dies
		Chester A. Arthur becomes president
1882	★	Congress approves a pension for all widows of U.S. presidents
1883	★	Congress passes the Pendleton Federal Civil Service Act, which reforms the way government jobs are given out
1884	★	Grover Cleveland is elected president
1886	★	Statue of Liberty is dedicated
1888	★	Benjamin Harrison is elected president
1892	★	Grover Cleveland is elected president
1896	★	William McKinley is elected president
1898	★	Battleship *Maine* explodes in Havana harbor, leading to the Spanish-American War
		United States annexes Puerto Rico, Guam, the Philippines, and Hawaii
1900	★	William McKinley is reelected president
1901	★	President McKinley is assassinated
		Theodore Roosevelt becomes president
1904	★	Theodore Roosevelt is elected president
1908	★	William Howard Taft is elected president
1909	★	National Association for Colored People (NAACP) is founded
1912	★	Woodrow Wilson is elected president
		Titanic sinks in the North Atlantic
1914	★	World War I begins
1916	★	Woodrow Wilson is reelected president
1917	★	United States enters World War I
1918	★	Lucretia Rudolph Garfield dies on March 14
		United States and its allies win World War I in November

Fast Facts about
Lucretia Rudolph Garfield

Born: April 19, 1832, in Garrettsville, Ohio

Died: March 14, 1918, in South Pasadena, California

Burial Site: Lake View Cemetery in Cleveland, Ohio

Parents: Zebulon Rudolph and Arabella Mason Rudolph

Education: Geauga Seminary (1848–1850) where she learned Latin, Greek, English, algebra, geometry, and science; Western Reserve Eclectic Institute (1850–1854) where she was the only woman to give a speech at her graduation

Career: Taught in a school in Chagrin Falls, Ohio; at Eclectic Institute in Hiram; and at schools in Ravenna, Ohio, and Cleveland, Ohio

Marriage: To James A. Garfield on November 11, 1858, until his death in 1881

Children: Elizabeth Arabella (1860–1863), Harry Augustus (1863–1942), James Rudolph (1865–1950), Mollie (1867–1947), Irvin McDowell (1870–1951), Abram (1872–1958), Edward (1874–1876)

Places She Lived: Garrretsville and Hiram, Ohio (1832–1864); Washington, D.C. (1864–1881); farm called Lawnfield in Mentor, Ohio (summers of 1876–1917); Cleveland, Ohio (1881–1917); Pasadena, California (many winters until March 14, 1918)

Major Achievements:

* Had just started making plans to redecorate the White House with historical accuracy when she became ill with malaria (May 1881).

* Showed great courage during the two months (July–September 1881) in which her husband was dying from the gunshot wounds of an assassin.

* Became the first First Lady to plan her husband's funeral and to appear in public for the funeral.

* At Lawnfield, organized her husband's letters and papers into the first memorial library for a U.S. president.

Fast Facts about
James A. Garfield's Presidency

Term of Office: Elected in 1880; served as the twentieth president of the United States from March 4, 1881, until September 19, 1881, when he died from gunshot wounds inflicted on July 2, 1881, by Charles J. Guiteau.

Vice President: Chester A. Arthur from March 4 to September 19, 1881; Arthur became the twenty-first president of the United States when Garfield died.

Major Policy Decisions and Legislation:

⋆ Appointed his cabinet (March 5–8, 1881), which included Abraham Lincoln's son Robert Todd Lincoln as secretary of war.

⋆ Gained the appointment of Stanley Matthews as an associate justice of the Supreme Court (March 12, 1881).

⋆ Gained the appointment of William H. Robertson, a political enemy of New York senator Roscoe Conkling, as collector of the Port of New York (May 18, 1881). This appointment caused Conkling to resign his Senate seat and may have added to Guiteau's reasons for wanting Garfield dead.

Where to Visit

The Capitol Building
Constitution Avenue
Washington, D.C. 20510
(202) 225-3121

James A. Garfield National Historic Site
8095 Mentor Avenue (U.S. 20)
Mentor, Ohio 44060
(440) 255-8722

Garfield Monument
Lake View Cemetery
Cleveland, Ohio

Museum of American History of the Smithsonian Institution
"First Ladies: Political and Public Image"
14th Street and Constitution Avenue NW
Washington, D.C.
(202) 357-2008

The National First Ladies Library
The Saxton McKinley House
331 South Market Avenue
Canton, Ohio 44702

White House
1600 Pennsylvania Avenue
Washington, D.C. 20500
Visitors' Office: (202) 456-7041

White House Historical Association
740 Jackson Place NW
Washington, D.C. 20503
(202) 737-8292

Online Sites of Interest

James A. Garfield National Historic Site

http://www.nps.gov/jaga/

A description of Lawnfield, the Garfield's large home in Mentor, Ohio, with its Memorial Library wing; includes information on area visitor attractions

The First Ladies of the United States of America

http://www2.whitehouse.gov/WH/glimpse/firstladies/html/firstladies.html

A portrait and biographical sketch of each First Lady plus links to other White House sites

History Happens

http://www.usahistory.com/presidents

A site that contains fast facts about James Garfield, including personal information and inaugural address

Internet Public Library, Presidents of the United States (IPL POTUS)

http://www.ipl.org/ref/POTUS/jagarfield.html

An excellent site with much information on James Garfield, including personal information and facts about his family and his presidency; inaugural address; many links to other sites including biographies and other internet resources

The National First Ladies Library

http://www.firstladies.org

The first virtual library devoted to the lives and legacies of America's First Ladies; includes a bibliography of books, articles, letters, and manuscripts by and about the nation's First Ladies; also includes a virtual tour, with pictures, of the Saxton McKinley House in Canton, Ohio, which houses the library

The White House

http://www.whitehouse.gov/WH/Welcome.html

Information about the current president and vice president; White House history and tours; biographies of past presidents and their families; a virtual tour of the historic building, current events, and much more

The White House for Kids

http://www.whitehouse.gov/WH/kids/html/kidshome.html

Includes information about White House children, past and present; famous "First Pets," past and present; historic moments of the presidency; and much more

For Further Reading

Chickamauga. Voices of the Civil War series. New York: Time Life Books, 1997.

Gormley, Beatrice. *First Ladies.* New York: Scholastic, Inc., 1997.

Gould, Lewis L. (ed.). *American First Ladies: Their Lives and Their Legacy.* New York: Garland Publishing, 1996.

Guzzetti, Paula. *The White House.* Parsippany, N.J.: Silver Burdett Press, 1995.

Klapthor, Margaret Brown. *The First Ladies.* 8th edition. Washington, D.C.: White House Historical Association, 1995.

Lillegard, Dee. *James A. Garfield.* Encyclopedia of Presidents. Chicago: Childrens Press, 1987.

Mayo, Edith P. (ed.). *The Smithsonian Book of the First Ladies: Their Lives, Times, and Issues.* New York: Henry Holt, 1996.

Paletta, Lu Ann. *World Almanac of First Ladies.* New York: World Almanac, 1990.

Shaw, John. *Crete and James: Personal Letters of Lucretia and James Garfield.* East Lansing, Mich.: Michigan State University Press, 1994.

Skarmeas, Nancy. *First Ladies of the White House.* Nashville, Tenn.: Ideals, 1995.

Index

Page numbers in **boldface type** indicate illustrations

Photo Identifications

Cover: Lucretia Rudolph Garfield portrait by Mathew Brady
Page 8: Mrs. James Abram Garfield (Lucretia)
Page 12: Lucretia's parents, Zebulon and Arabella Rudolph
Page 22: Hiram College (formerly called the Western Reserve Eclectic Institute), Hiram, Ohio
Page 36: Ohio State Capitol, Columbus
Page 48: James A. Garfield and his daughter Mollie, 1870
Page 64: James A. Garfield, official portrait as president
Page 88: Lucretia in her later years

Photo Credits©

About the Author

Ann Heinrichs grew up in Arkansas and lives in Chicago. She has written over twenty books on American, Asian, and African history and culture, as well as numerous newspaper, magazine, and encyclopedia articles. In the advertising and marketing fields, her subjects have ranged from plumbing hardware to Oriental rugs. Besides the United States, she has traveled in Europe, North Africa, the Middle East, and east Asia. The desert is her favorite terrain. Ms. Heinrichs holds bachelor's and master's degrees in piano performance. For serenity, she practices chi gung, t'ai chi, and ritual sword forms.